Advance Praise for
Delightenment

"Awe inspiring, miraculous, a great achievement. *Delightenment* is full of profound wisdom and life-changing insights. Everyone should read this book. It will rock your world."

    —John Gray, Author
    Men are from Mars, Women are from Venus

"You have in your hands a miracle ~ a book that has been brewing for decades in the brilliant mind and huge heart of Neal Rogin, one of our planet's most enlightened human beings who has been gifted all his life with a rare kind of genius. This book is so beautiful it will bring you to tears. Every word has power and magic in it. This is a book that you will keep with you always. You will quote it, feel it, love it, and hopefully embody its profound message.

"It is as lighthearted as it is deep, as joyful as it is challenging, and as timely as it is timeless. Give yourself the gift of this message. It will bless your life."

    —Lynne Twist, Author
    The Soul of Money

"*Delightenment* is not just a book. It is a new way to see our world. It is a wisdom revolution. It is a call to action to transform our culture in a way that everyone I know wants our society to evolve."

    —Dave Ellis, Facilitator and Coach
    Author, *Falling Awake*

Delightenment

To my wife, Diane
my muse, Fay
and my teacher, Miranda

Dear Brother Michael,

May this renaissance of connection celebrate the beautiful energies we came to share + deliver! I love you always

Delightenment

ESCAPING THE SOLITARY CONFINEMENT OF YOUR PRISONALITY

NEAL ROGIN

Delightenment Press
Novato, California

Delightenment Press
2204 Laguna Vista Drive
Novato, CA 94945

To order copies go to: **Delightenmentbook.com**

Cover design by Brooks Cole
Cover image: Magnetosphere, the magnetic shield that protects Earth from intense solar radiation. ©Joe Menth, made using Uniview for StoryDome.org.

Delightenment/**Neal Rogin**.—1st ed.
ISBN 978-06929791-6-7

*The Light at the end of the tunnel
is a mirror.*

Table of Contents

Introduction

The purpose of this book is to help redefine what it means to be human. To enable us to distinguish the existence of our ego identity and gain a measure of freedom from its tyranny. And in doing so find ourselves increasingly free from the constellation of fear, pain and suffering that is called "the Human Condition."

Outcomes:
- A sense of calm wellbeing, a grounded optimism and feeling of safety, congruence and coherence.

- A knowing sense that "I belong here."

- Clarity, equanimity and sobriety when confronting life's challenges, whether personally in our families and our work, or globally as environmental destruction and social injustices.

- Freedom from the lifelong ingrained patterns of fear, judgment, indifference, anger and despair that interfere with the enjoyment of life.

This book is not intended to fix anyone, but to help us awaken from the dream that we need to be fixed.

Delightenment is based on several assumptions, among them:

- The world is not what it appears to be. We are not who we assume ourselves to be. We have fallen under a spell, an enchantment, a kind of dream, in which we each experience ourselves as a "me," a separate entity, apart from everyone and everything.

- The person we think we are is a fiction that we keep alive by attempting to find and fix what is wrong with it. As long as we identify with this inner commentary, we don't have thoughts, our thoughts have us.

- We consider ourselves as a problem to be solved. We experience a constant yearning to find and mend what is broken in us and desire to fill an unnamable emptiness that we mistakenly contextualize as "me." What is a "me?" It is a separate identity, an id-entity, a self-sustaining, self-justifying, self-referential mental conversation generated by an unquestioned belief that this "me" is real. It is who I am.

- If we don't distinguish our deep Self from the voice in our head, life will be an endless wild goose chase, a ceaseless marathon in search of a solution to the problem of "me." Seek and ye shall seek.

Chapter Zero

Someday it will be known as the Great Hippie Migration of the late 1960's, and I was swept up in its tidal power. I left my old life behind in Chicago, and arrived in San Francisco in the fall of 1967, missing the Summer of Love by a few months. Things were cooling down a bit by then. The Summer of Love had become the Autumn of Like.

I had recently quit my job as a Midwest Mad Man writing clever headlines designed to persuade homemakers about the benefits of serving Betty Crocker Brownies to their kids, and came to San Francisco searching for I didn't know what. I had happily severed any connection I still had to my former life, and flipped the Bird to the Establishment, and stuck it to The Man. And why not? The Revolution was now well underway and total victory was just around the corner. What could possibly go wrong?

Well, as we all now know, the 60's turned out not to be The Revolution but rather a kind of opening night party to celebrate the beginning of The Revolution, which would actually take a little longer than expected.

My next few years were spent taking round trips to paradise on an LSD-fueled bus. It was a very important time in my life, but in retrospect it was a stage, not a destination. Psychedelics had shown me a reality beyond the one I thought was the only reality. But taking a round trip vacation to Heaven and always returning to ordinary me was getting old. I did not want to visit paradise anymore; I wanted to emigrate. So I became a spiritual seeker.

This led me to many spiritual teachers, among them was a man named Charles Berner.

During the 1960's Berner invented a process he called an Enlightenment Intensive. It promised to provide anyone a state of spiritual enlightenment in a few days. Right up my alley. It combined the self-enquiry meditation method popularized by the Indian saint Ramana Marharshi, with the dyad structure of co-counseling. Seekers like me were supported in maintaining a single-pointed focus for three full days and nights on one unanswerable question: "Who am I?" From early morning to the wee hours, we would sit dyad style while our partner said, "Tell me who you are." And we would endeavor to inquire deeply into the very nature our true self, by asking who was asking "Who am I?" What is the true nature of him who seeks, of this consciousness? Who is asking? And who just asked that?

Here it was Monday morning, after a weekend of fiercely wondering nothing but who was asking who am I. I had experienced a few authentic and deep spiritual insights, and moments of absolute peace, but nothing I would define as genuine Enlightenment. Not that I knew what that was, but I knew if I had to ask, "am I enlightened?" I wasn't.

In those days I had what I considered the perfect counter culture job: manager of a leather store on Grant Avenue in San Francisco's North Beach, a bustling melting pot of beatnik coffee houses, hippie hang outs, Italian restaurants, Chinese laundries and the latest phenomenon, topless bars. The most famous of these was the Condor Club featuring one miss Carol Doda, whose enormous augmented cleavage was so iconic that columnist Herb Caen would later dub them "Silicone Valley."

I was preparing to open the store for the day. As I pushed the broom across the old wooden floorboards, I was still deeply engrossed in the process of self-inquiry. "Who is sweeping?" I thought. "Who wants to know who is sweeping? Who just asked who wants to know who wants to know…." Just then I looked up and caught a glimpse of myself in the mirror, not a regular mirror, mind you, but a three-way. So I saw myself from the side, as if I were someone else.

Now, I don't know if what I did next had anything to do with what was about to happen, but it's all I have for an explanation. Here I was with the broom, asking the question from a place of not knowing. The guy in the mirror, I suddenly realized, was not asking the question; he was *creating* the question. That may seem like a distinction without a difference, but bear with me.

Asking the question brings into being the assumption of not knowing. The one asking only asks because he does not know. To ask is to be the seeker. One who creates the question, however is in a state of non-duality, holding both the seeker and the answer at once.

Anyway, it really doesn't matter, because what happened next changed everything forever.

How do I put words to this? Let's start by saying I was struck by a bolt of divine lightning. Kaboom! In a micro second, a massively blissful, glorious, gorgeous, burst of ecstatic energy knocked me to the ground, where I found myself weeping and repeating over and over again "Thank you, thank you, thank you." It was not like any spiritual breakthrough, or drug induced euphoric journey or orgasm. In fact, it was unlike any experience I ever had or hope to have. Because it did not happen within my own sensorium, within what I consider to be "me" where every thought, insight, dream, idea, occurs. There is no other realm. Or so I assumed.

In truth, it was not something that I experienced. It was more like an experience that had me.

What happened next was equally astonishing. I pulled myself to my feet. The leather shop had transformed into a kind of amphitheater, like an operating theater. I could sense that beings were present, looking down at me. I started to speak. Well, it was not what I considered to be "me" but another consciousness. It delivered through me more than an hour of the most coherent, insightful and inspiring truths, none of which I remember. I only remember a tiny part of the "me" that had not been obliterated thinking, "this is good stuff."

This phenomenon was clearly the most significant event of my life. And has remained so to this day. For weeks afterward, I lived in an enchanted world. For example, when I listened to classical music, say a Mozart Symphony, I would hear lyrics, sung by what seemed a choir of angels. Lyrics so beautiful, so inspiring, so true, that I would be brought to tears. If this was not a direct experience of the Divine, it was God enough for me.

Eventually, the enchantment subsided, leaving only an afterglow, and an attempt by my ordinary consciousness to reassert itself. I went through a long period of denial, rationalization and confusion. There simply was no way to explain what had happened. It did not fit into any of my frames of reference. It was as if God had parted the curtain on this play and said "Peekaboo! None of what you know, and how you know it, is real. This glory, this majesty, this unutterable splendor ~ this is real." My ordinary day-to-day existence took on a kind of shadow play unreality. It was now a challenge to take anything, any event, any content of what I had called my life seriously. It was now just a passing show, a three-dimensional theatrical event. All I wanted was to understand the dynamics of the reality hidden behind what I had considered to be the real world. I wondered: If this thunderclap of pure glory had come in response to my feverish quest to know who I am, could other questions be answered from the same mysterious source? If I inquired deeply, sincerely, humbly seeking to penetrate to the heart of wisdom, would this wisdom respond? In other words, if this profound spiritual lightning bolt that knocked me down (and broke me open) in the leather shop that morning marked the opening of some kind of channel to the Divine, was that channel still open?

So I sat down in front of a blank page with an open mind, a humble heart and my pen in hand. And for the first time, wrote a simple question that has become a key that has unlocked what is for me a treasure trove of spiritual insight, guidance and wisdom: "What is the truth here, now please?" Every time I would ask this question, a voice would answer. And every time it spoke to me, I wrote down what it said. Invariably after capturing its message with pen and paper, I would hide it away ~ in a drawer, on a shelf, in a file. I told almost no one about this phenomenon, or about the storehouse of deep wisdom I had squirreled away.

Maybe I felt that it would make me seem like some kind of weirdo. Only certifiable nuts hear voices. Crazy people, serial killers, mad men. The Son of Sam, Jeffery Daumer, Homer Simpson. Also, the ideas this Other was presenting while often humorous, were radical, revolutionary, even disturbing. They were also profoundly liberating.

For the first time in my life, I experienced being addressed not as "me" but as that which lies behind "me." It was not speaking to my ego. It was speaking *about* it, revealing its secrets, exposing its tricks, showing me the sophisticated structure of self-deception, self-preservation and domination behind what I had always considered to be "me." And with each revelation, each teaching, one aspect of this complex of conclusions and decisions that made up my personality dropped away.

Over the years the distinction between my ego identity and this Other has become increasingly transparent. My sense that I am a somebody named Neal, separate and distinct from all the other somebodies, while still very much present, has become something I have, rather than someone I am. I see my ego now more like a fictional character I have been playing in this comedy/drama called

My Life. (Starring the commentator in my head, featuring my thoughts as written by my misunderstandings of the events of the plot thus far. Produced by my parents in partnership with my schoolteachers, rabbis and other assorted and wildly misguided mentors.)

Let's be clear. I am a professional writer. My writing is all about craft, about rewriting and revising. My motto when I am blocked is, "Make a mistake in the direction of your intention." So I draft something that looks awful, sounds terrible, maybe even feels embarrassing. Then I rewrite it, revise it, slowly improve it, maybe find the one sentence that is kind of acceptable. I add a phrase here, substitute a better word there. At some point the draft actually stops looking not so terrible and starts to look pretty good, and eventually maybe even becomes something great.

But when this wisdom is present, there is no rewriting, no hesitation, no second thoughts. It flows like a stream, first filling my mind then running down my arm, into the pen and onto the paper. And always with elegant language, precise vocabulary, wry irony, surprising twists. It comes to me whole cloth. Not a word is out of place, not a thought of revision. And almost always it comes in answer to my request for help when I feel stuck. It never fails to correct my confusion, resolve my upset, illuminate my misunderstanding. And always gently, without making anything wrong; it is kind, gentle, forgiving and spacious. After each encounter I feel not just relieved but reminded, exonerated, released, and known. The word that most describes my feeling after reading one of these gems, is delight.

For a long time, I struggled with the usual ego-based questions: Where is this coming from? Am I the author? Or is God? But none of that matters anymore. I now understand that I am and always have been a scribe, a curator and a custodian. I have been given a great gift, but the gift is not mine to keep; it was given to me to be given to others.

Please understand, I am not pretending that what I have been privy to is anything new. It is the same ancient wisdom that all the great seers, sages and saints have been teaching for centuries. It is, however, a new and I think powerful and accessible perspective on the eternal truths of the spiritual journey. Not a new testament, but more of a *now* testament. In that sense, it is potentially revolutionary.

What you hold in your hands are the fruits of a lifelong relationship between "me" and the great I-don't-know-what, a non-physical mysterious wisdom source that has never let me down, never failed to illuminate my understanding of life's mysteries, or explain my confusion, my fears, my dark moods in a way that brought light and love into my experience of living a human life.

All of these teachings came in response to questions extremely personal to me, specific guidance for my particular challenges. Hopefully, you will also find them useful on your journey.

WARNING!
Dangerous Ideas Ahead.
May be hazardous to your worldview.
Proceed with caution.

The source of the visible is invisible.

We come from the invisible spectrum of love,
and manifest into the visible spectrum of light.

Light is love looked upon and seen.

Light is love slowed down enough to become visible.
The essence of all reality is love in motion.

The only thing faster than the speed of light
is the speed of love.

It is instantaneous.

Speed is infinite when something simply is.
Love is. There is no distance when love is.

Speed is a function of separation.
Separation is an illusion.
No separation, no time, no speed.

Love moves at the ultimate velocity.

Godspeed

Prisonality

When you are enchanted by the external world you made, you are fixated only on one thing: to get from the external world what you refuse to give to yourself: acceptance, admiration, understanding, trust, confidence, validation, respect, love.

When you ask the world for what you withhold from your self, you become a prisoner locked inside a fear-driven reality that you yourself are projecting, like a dimensional hologram emanating from you, the spherical projector and amnesiac audience.

You forsake your awareness of your authorship in order to experience a reality in which you are at the effect of events that appear to be external to you and not of your doing.

To God, this is a very interesting experience.

The question is...

Will you allow me to enter your reality and be what you are in the world? If you will step aside ~ give up your personal history ~ stop trying to make sense, to have meaning, to add up to something ~ if you will give up trying to make your life story turn out, I can come.

I can be here, with you, as you. But for me to be here, you must go, willingly, purposefully, eyes openly, voluntarily.

Can you let go of your story? Can you dispose of years of struggle and terror? Can you extinguish your need to validate, exonerate, justify or vindicate your self and your history ~ and just let the historical, hysterical (your name here) go?

Can you finally stop pretending so hard that you are not something bad? Can you give up protesting your innocence, withdraw your not guilty plea?

Can you let go forever of the structure you have created to solve your misunderstanding ~ your assumption of the loss of love, of the absence of your creator, of your separation from your experience of your life?

You labor so hard to assuage your abandonment. You deny it. You rail against it. You pretend to be beyond it. You pretend to accept it. Then you carefully build a clever ruse to get around it.

You wall off a small segment of your totality ~ a kind of ritual cosmetic amputation ~ to accommodate the resignation to the inevitability of your predicament; marooned in life, on a ball of dirt in the middle of nowhere, trapped on a cold, desolate, isolated island in a dark and frigid universe.

What a crock! You have gone into a theater to watch a horror movie, and while there got knocked on the head, got amnesia, woke up and now think the movie is real. You went into that theater long ago. Time to come out now. Ali ali oxen free! It is just a movie. Really.

Amnesia[2]

I see you standing with your electrical cord in your hand, powerless unless you plug into something or someone outside of you. There is no experience of the power source that is within you. This is the classic disempowerment of the civilized modern human.

The power is turned off within and so power and authority must be sought without. Thus everything, including the church and religion, love and drama, the arts ~ all human yearnings.

Turning this trick of making the source forget its own nature so that it is weak and seeks solace from that which is its own creation and from those who are its own servants ~ this is the dark purpose of what is called education. Every meta-message, every dark and debilitating mantra that is drilled into the mind of a human being to make him Homo ignoramus ~ reduces the light and deepens the darkening of the illusion we live in ~ the massive misunderstanding under which we labor.

The Great Forgetting. Amnesia[2].

So I say remember that you know; recall that you forgot. Resist the hidden onslaught that reinforces your misunderstanding. Regain clear access to the truth you have never ceased to be.

Don't inflate the importance of the shortcomings you discover in the *prisonality* of this present current time. (Your name here) is merely the shape of your accommodation to your perception that love is scarce and God is dead. Remember ~ you are not the person you're pretending not to be.

Fear is the stranger here. This is love's abode. You are not alone. You are loved and known and welcomed and wanted. You don't know this because you're the only one who cannot have you in his life. You cannot know you as others know you because you are you.

Be glad ~ not sorry ~ to be here.
Celebrate ~ not regret ~ that you were born.
Embrace ~ not avoid ~ the world you encounter.
It is your canvas.
You are an artist.
Paint your truth.
Write your love.
Sing your self!

Creation is digital.

There is only nothing
and One...

Various patterns and
manifestations of being
and nothingness.

Light and shadow.
Presence, absence.
On, off.

The flicker of reality.
We supply the continuity
by tying it together in a story.

We make "sense" of the individual
moments of now.

You are yourself

Once you experience you are God,
you don't experience being God.
You experience being yourself,
and loving it.

And you listen to all the people
who don't experience being themselves,
trying their damnedest to experience being God.

You can never become an idea.
You are the source of ideas.
You are the source of the idea
that there are such things as ideas.

You are not "God." You are yourself. There is no other.
God is simply what the sleeping call the awakened.

Telling the ego "you are God" makes it crazy.

When you make something that is already crazy
Crazy, it disappears, revealing that you are God.

Big deal.

Conclusion-Jumping ought to be an Olympic sport.

Almost all an ego does
is add meaning to every event.
Something happens, and
we make it mean something.

By adding meaning we lock ourselves
into the individual, solitary confinement
of our (perceived) cell of separation.

By making meaning we create the illusion ~
the mirage ~ that we are not each other.

How do you like me now?

Where are we today?
Are we getting present to the actuality
of the wisdom that has been guiding you?
Or do you still intend to pretend you are not _that_?
That you are at best nobody and at worst a bungling
victim, a loser, clueless and confused ~ not to be taken
seriously ~ dismissible and unimportant?

In other words, are you still hiding?
Hiding behind your pretense of ineptitude
that is your struggling ego self?

What fear do you have that keeps your heart
hidden from us in the cave of your privacy?

What fear you?
It looks over its shoulder to see if we are watching,
wondering what we're thinking, hungering to manage our
thoughts, seeking to remotely control our experience of
itself.

They call it "Seeking outside validation
as a source of self-esteem."

We call it Opinion Management.
And it is a lousy career choice.

Why do you fear awakening?

It is only your fear of being without fear ~
of being in a state where fear is irrelevant and unnecessary.

Your fear perpetuates itself. It is really the _state_ ~
the chemical/physical/emotional/intellectual array flooding
your consciousness ~ that is the content of your
experience that you have become addicted to.

The Fear Rush (which because it has become virtually
continuous is no longer a rush but rather a hum
you call your life.)

You _choose_ it. You make the fear choice ~
out of habit and addiction.

You are not afraid. You are choosing to experience the
effects of responding to exterior events out of fear. You
are pushing the fear button to have it release the
chemicals that trigger the feeling of "Uh-oh."

That is scary.

Reality is reality.

The way you feel about that fact
determines the quality
of your life.

If you make reality wrong
you are casting yourself in a whodunit
in which you dunit and don't know it.

You create reality,
then pretend to be smaller than your creation,
maintaining the pretense by making reality wrong.

You animate an alligator
then pretend to wrestle with him ~ and *lose*!
And then you use your creativity to conjure reasons
to justify your defeat.

Come now.

It goes without saying...

The ego speaks
when you have nothing to say
and speak anyway.

And the best it does
is make no difference
and the worst it does
is kill what you love.

The truth will fill the silence
when you leave unsaid
what needn't be uttered.

The truth resides in silence.
It reveals itself in the emptiness
left by the refraining from expressing
that which needn't be said.

The truth lives in emptiness.

Make more Nothing.

You think your secrets make you special.

What we withhold from others keeps us from knowing our connected transcendent unity.

The truth of our oneness is obscured by the lie of our separation, reinforced and held in place by the secrets we think we keep.

We feel our unknown places, our private thoughts, our pettiness, can be used as a refuge from being completely seen ~ and therefore distinct, therefore alone.

Know you are utterly known, understood,
seen, and utterly loved. You have no secrets
to conceal, no sinfulness to reveal.

All is known ~ all is forgiven.
All is as before, restored to innocence
by being discovered to have been eternally unblemished.

You are Consciousness, aware of its true nature,
located in this dimensional space time...
Knowingness knowing it knows.
Consciousness conscious of its consciousness.

So? Just say know.

The Power of Not Now.

Why is your ego self, your Me, so fearful of Now,
of the actual present moment?

It seems its three operating rules are
1) Not here.
2) Not now.
3) Not me.

So the avoidance of being present in time or in space, and
the absolute refusal to be in any way responsible for
anything that happens, is its primary function.

If not now, when? The ego says, "Later."
If not here, where? "Over there."
If not you, who? "That guy."

Your ego must at all cost not let the present moment
come to consciousness, because it does not exist Here
and cannot exist Now. It can only exist, or appear to exist,
in the lie of later, over there, with that guy.

Now is its enemy. Here is its undoing.
And Me? Well, that's the biggest surprise of all.
Turns out your sense of Me is a fictional character you
keep alive by trying to become a better person.

You are not a person.

Telling Time

When you tell time,
what do you tell it?
And does it ever listen?
"I wish I was back in college."
"When will my vacation start?"

Stop telling time
and it will become
less real to you,
less your master.

It's okay to keep track,
but stop telling time.

Remember:
Time is not passing by;
it's running in place.

Beware.

Your ego structure, your identity,
your limited sense of self,
your defining context
has to limit your scope of experience.
It has to restrict the level of being you can allow.

Your definition of yourself as just "me"
means there are things that this "me"
cannot allow to be known.
There must be a consistency of identity.
That means you must project your experience
through a filter that determines the shape
of what you allow yourself to know you know.

Who you are is really a measure
of what you allow yourself to know you know.

You know?

Ego Redundancy

Your validity as a person is not in question
every time you are called on to do the work.

The work is not a test.
It is a privilege.

You do not need to
dip deep into doubt
to retrieve the answer.

The work is not a burden.
It is a gift. To be born lightly and given freely.

Your ego makes the work difficult
in an effort to discredit God.

Grace makes the ego redundant.
Why would you need protection
against something that loves you?

When you are afraid, you have forgotten.

You have been captivated, trying to solve a problem
that is not real.

Your attempt to solve it is the investment
with which you make it seem real.

You really are the projector
frightened by your own projections.

Do not try to fix the image on the screen.
Focus yourself.

You are mistaking God
for your enemy.

Look again.

Hope and Fear

Things (you for example)
are never as good as you hope
or as bad as you fear.

Because hope and fear
dwell in the domain of duality.
You are something else entirely ~ a singularity.

You are incomparable.

DELIGHTENMENT

The World of the Sleeptalkers

Who cares what they argue about.
Taking sides in the world of duality
takes you away from the "All" ~ the one side
which has no other side.
The Single Good,
the Only Light,
the One Source ~
God.

Seek the unity,
for unity transcends your consciousness.
When you become aware of awareness ~
when you become conscious of consciousness,
then you can transcend the duality
become un-fascinated,
break the fixation,
finally become dis-enchanted.

The spell is broken, the bubble bursts
and you fall awake.

NEAL ROGIN

Suddenly the struggle upward to become
even more singularly, separately successful,
as the brilliant animal atop the
Great Pyramid of Creation, where
the room to be becomes less and less
the closer you get to singular perfection
(which is unattainable yet ever pursuable) gives way…

You come to ~
and find yourself standing at the gateway of
a golden bridge, one that widens as you walk it
until it becomes Everything, which is what you are.

Now the singular search for personal perfection
has become the spontaneous surrendering to the ever-
expanding experience of the love of God.

You are eternal

Your life story, your total allegiance to the content of your consciousness, your commitment to the continuity of your identity as an individual "me," your preoccupation with its travails and triumphs, all this is a trance, a spell, an enchantment. You ~ your "me" ~ is an apparition, an image on a scrim, a stage trick, a ghost. The only thing that makes it seem so real is your continual fixation, truly your unending need to fix it, to mess with your made-up self, to fine tune your imaginary friend, to get it right.

Your memoir, your three-act play, your biopic is being written by you as you go along. Most of the plot is based on what happened in the previous chapters, avoiding the mistakes of, improving on, regretting what we call the past. So for those of you who are smack in the middle of that epic entitled "Life as Me" ~ Spoiler alert! The hero dies at the end.

Your person-ness, your "prisonality," your sense of that "me" that you think yourself to be is a reality show in which you are the central character and also the biggest fan. The show will come to an end, the last page of the script will be written and read, the curtain will come down, the credits will roll, but you, the you that has been here all along thinking of itself as "me," that you, will remain. That you cannot die. That you is eternal. Let me say it this way: You are eternal.

I'd like to exchange this please.

If you find yourself in God's general store, standing in the return line with your life in your hands, hoping to trade it in for something better, you are in the wrong line. This is it. And by now, it's no secret. Unconditional acceptance is key to the freedom, happiness and peace of mind we all are after. No mystery here. Choose what is.

This is improv, baby. We are all are making this up as we go along. The secret of successful improvisational acting is simple: accept what is happening and build on it. It's called "yes, and…" Whatever life puts before you, choose that. Rather than judging it, or trying to change it, or wish things were different, say "yes, and…" That means accept it, go with it, add to it, include it as if it was already in your plans. Do not make it wrong. You don't have to like it. Just don't conclude that it shouldn't be happening.

Resist resisting. Accept acceptance. Judge the judge. Doubt your doubts. And let what happens be uncontested by you. Your role is not to judge reality. You are not here to second-guess God. Receive, accept, allow, surrender, relinquish control, climb into the passenger seat. Ride shotgun and let God drive. And see what happens.

Much of your psychological pain is most likely a result of resisting the way it is. Arguing with the flow of reality. If you were at a movie and suddenly the plot turned dark, would you storm to the box office and demand your money back? Of course not. You are here to enjoy the show.

DELIGHTENMENT

Beloved One, know this:

All is in the great hands of the Creator of All.
Darkness ~ the absence not the opposite of light ~
though prevalent, is not real, but an illusion ~
a horror film we project on the screen
in the theater of our mind.

Mind itself is an illusion,
better yet, a creation, a construct of being,
by Being to be able to re-cognize what Being cognates, for
the recognition of cognition.

The screen in the theater is a construct
upon which the Being bestows its locus of identity,
wherein the screen itself is identified as the self
and the flickering images (made of pictures, emotions,
decisions, thoughts and feelings) become
"what's happening" and "my life."
And the Being is drawn spellbound
into a fascination with the illusion
that its survival can be threatened.

This is the spell that must be broken.
The great dis-enchantment to thus transform
the self-identity of the human being
from Human to _Being_.

There are only reasons not to enjoy.

All reasons explain the absence of God.
There is no explanation for God.

There's no reason to be happy,
Except life itself.

Being is happy.
Being and Joy are one.
Get to being and you will be in joy.
Get to joy and you'll be being.

Being is reasonless, unexplainable, indescribable.

It is not a destination
Or another place.

At the level of cognition, of origination,
Being sustains reality.

Nothing sustains being.
Only Nothing sustains being.

Up to You

You can live as if you are at stake,
and be engrossed in the narrative linear
history of events in which "you" are
embedded as a character in a story
as it unfolds...

or

You can withdraw your total acceptance of the
reality of suffering and fear, and live as you are...
As Nothing at all. A roiling ball of process and change,
held in a setting of pure singular unchanging
un-begun and never-ending perfection.

Your choice.

Wait...What?

It is not that you lack that causes you to seek.
It is that you have an excess. You have not less,
but more than what you need.

What you have and don't need
is the idea that there is something you lack.

You have too much of an idea
that you don't have enough.

You need not improve.
You only need to awaken
from the dream that says
I need to improve.

Dreaming danger

You remain embroiled in your role as your small self by not confronting what you would require of yourself to do if you saw through to the truth of your real self.

What stitches you into your identity is the primary lie you believe of yourself that you are lost, broken. That life is dangerous, reality cruel, the universe a place of menace and terror. You perpetuate this recurring group nightmare to avoid the light and love that is your birthright and within which you are always embedded, enfolded and embraced in eternal safety and infinite security.

There is only love. And that is frightening to your belief in darkness. So you conjure a reality of challenge and suffering, when in truth ~ you are asleep in the palm of God's hand, dreaming danger.

More than meets the eye

When you think that what is going on
is all that's going on, you are lost.
When you think that the content of your life ~
the story of you ~ is *you*, then you are adrift.

When you realize, even for an instant,
that there is much, much more to you
than meets the eye, you begin your journey.

Then you start to seek to remember who you have
forgotten, and to forget who you have up to now,
considered yourself to be.

Fixing the fool

There is, you think, an existence to which you have given valence. This apparition is a continual creation to which you have given identity and mass. It is considered by you to be you.

It does not exist. And your preoccupation with its improvement and its eventual triumph over the forces that oppose it, is a fiction.

The conflict and controversy do not exist. Your continual attempt to resolve yourself is all you can do in a reality that says you are not real, and your apparition, your dilemma, is. The very attempt to free yourself puts you in prison.

Any effort directed at solving your dilemma is an attempt to prove your helplessness. You are not helpless. You are able. So able, in fact, that you are even able to pretend that you are helpless, and to make it real. Only one as able as this could disarm oneself of all ability.

Your preoccupation with your own salvation is the last block to your true salvation ~ the realization of your own eternal safety.

You are fooling yourself and trying to fix the fool.
There is no fixing, for there is no fool.
There is no escape, because there is no imprisonment.
There is no way out, because there are no walls.

Life is a Chinese Finger Puzzle.

Shadow chasing

Ego, Devil, Satan, Darkness
are the names of the shadow
who thinks he lives.

The assumption of separate life.

The shadow is never separate
from the light by which it is cast.

The shadow is absence,
not presence.

Absence does not have a separate
and distinct existence.

Absence is not presence.

We have been empowering non-existence.
We have been following absence,
chasing our shadow,
knowing all the while that
the light must be around here somewhere.

The absence of light has no power.
Unless you give it yours.

The Knowing-Action Cycle

What follows knowing is action.
If action does not ensue from knowing,
what is known as experience becomes remembered as
belief. And sleep is the result.

This slumber is a product of the incompletion of the
knowledge-action cycle. This is the source of self-doubt
and the subsequent need to prove one's validity ~ the
mechanism we call the ego.

Self-doubt (ergo ego) is a justification for not being willing
to know the truth. It is the confusion that we conjure to
avoid the action that clarity would require and integrity
demand.

It is somehow more comfortable
to choose to remain ignorant of the problem
than to know exactly what the problem is
and take no action to solve it.

From the point of view of the Self,
all unconsciousness, all confusion, all limitation
is merely the unwillingness to confront the consequences
of knowing the truth.

The lyrics to your song of fear

Dwelling on shortcomings and fearful possibilities serves no purpose and disables your natural ability to respond. You cannot scare yourself into action. You cannot ultimately motivate yourself by fear and panic and the avoidance of pain.

Fear freezes, leaves you powerless, because in that condition (of panic, fear, avoidance) you cannot possibly see the natural way through. In fear, you don't know what to do next, and when you do act, since it comes out of fear, it is ineffective, which makes you think *you* are ineffective, which makes you more fearful, and so on.

Remember, the voice that explains why you should be afraid ~ the lyric for your song of fear ~ is always seductive, always makes perfect sense. You cannot argue with the voice of fear. Just don't engage. Don't listen to yourself when you are afraid. Don't entertain the conversation.

The truth is, you have nothing to fear. Knowing you have nothing to fear is not enough to stop you from fearing. The habit ~ the reaction to your nightmare ~ is strong.

You are terrified of shadows on the wall cast by your misconceptions. Don't ask for salvation. Don't ask to be saved from the shadows of your misunderstanding. Don't ask to be protected. Ask only to be awakened from your feverish dream.

To offer salvation as you understand it, is to further your imprisonment within the dream.

The radical personal declaration of independence

Nobody owns your consciousness. Nobody owns your ability to choose. You give it away; you abdicate. You let life tell you what is real and who you are in the matter. You take life's version of your story. But the story is just a piece of software. It is not hardwired. It can be rewritten.

How you construe reality, where you stand when you think, your unexamined assumptions about what is real and what is not, what is possible and what is not, who you are and who you are not ~ all of that is malleable, changeable. The Story that explains all things, the conclusion you have reached given the facts you have collected, is based on a limited set of those facts. You don't have all the facts, never have, but always have constructed a reality as if, at that time, you knew everything. You did not know everything. Never have known everything. And you do not know everything now.

The arrogance of human consciousness lies here, where it constructs a story that explains reality in light of a limited set of facts. This story is constructed as if it explains all the facts, the assumption being that there are no new facts, the knowing of which might change the story.

The story you tell now is that you are a creature. But not just an ordinary creature. You give your lowly station a grandiosity by construing yourselves as The Chosen Creature. The favored child of the Creator.

You are not creation's most brilliant animal...

…You are its most ignorant God.

Lighter than error

The things in your life you believe
are propping you up,
are holding you down.

You are a balloon,
not a rock.
If you let go
You will fall up.

Let go.
Fall awake.

Pretending to forget

Relax.

Take comfort in the unshakeable bedrock reality
that all is well and all shall be well.

Thou art That.

The only control "you" have is illusory,
to pretend that you are not That.

Know it is simply impossible to not,
already and always,
be who you are.

It is only possible to temporarily pretend to forget.

The wall of thought

Quiet your self-talk so you can perceive the peace that
always waits behind the insubstantial illusion created by
your ego's fears projecting onto your wall of thought.

Take refuge in the eternal safety of
the Present Moment.

Rest in the ever presence.

Where you really come from

No matter how much worldly success you have achieved,
way down in your bones you know that there is much more
to you than you've shown so far.

Like so many of us, you feel a deep yearning
to bring something vital, something uniquely yours
to the suffering world.

No amount of outward achievement, no amount of fame,
kudos or accolades can fill this yearning to transcend your
empty and separate sense of "me" and deliver to our
world what you came here to give.

You've had glimpses of a shimmering reality
behind our fractured and suffering world.
A golden honey colored realm of pure peace, absolute
acceptance, pure love.

It's where you really come from.
It's who you really are.

The door to that sacred reality opens inward.
It can be found in only one place:
The Present Moment.

Nothing doing

In the realm below being,
in the realm of re-cognition, awareness,
in the realm of thought-process-action-results ~
the fear of doing it wrong, keeps you in inaction,
which itself is action.

It takes more doing to do nothing.

The energy you exert by holding back
is greater by far than the energy to surrender.

It takes a lot of effort not to care.

The Escape

The way is open.

You have discovered the key to the Great Secret
that allowed you to unlock the gate.
That secret: The gate was never locked.

The question now is:
will you stand in front of the prison
from which you have discovered yourself released
(having never been incarcerated in the first place)
and throw stones at the walls?

It's tempting to dwell on what you used to think was so.
No need.

Put your foot firmly on the path that leads you know not
where. And leave the comfort of your enslavement, the
certainty of your chains, where they belong ~ in the story
you made up called your "life" and in the non-existent
echoes of events you totally misunderstood called your
"past."

Leave that all behind.
Leave being predictable behind.
Leave having any idea what anything really is, behind.

Dare to wonder as if you know nothing,
and to listen as if you can know everything.

Just because it feels real, does not make it so.

Notice the background noise.

A slight feeling of impending, oh I don't know, DOOM!

The foundational ground of fear, like a coat of paint on the floor of your consciousness. A kind of post-traumatic echo, an element of the so-called human condition.

A kind of remnant of the Big Bang of your disconnected moment, your separation from God, when you found yourself suddenly and most apparently a separate distinct isolated individual, born only to die alone.

Really?

Who made you the judge?

You can never really change something
if you make it wrong.

Acceptance precedes power.

A judge is impotent.

If you demand the power to judge creation,
you abdicate your power to move it.

A self-appointed judge
is a disappointed self.

What's missing

What would life be like if you weren't run by fear? If you didn't fixate on your external "reality" for reassurance, for guidance, for clues, so you know what to want? You know what you want! You want what God wants, the continual and unceasing unfolding of the Divine Idea on Earth.

There is no answer in others, no solace in any external source. The world holds nothing you need. It needs what you bring. Time to stop pretending you don't know this. Time to stop being kind to the blind by poking out your own eyes to make them comfortable. As if they possess something critical that you do not possess, and desperately need. Again, the external world is here to be served, loved, corrected, and perfected by you.

There is nothing missing in you.
You are what's missing in the world.

The tyranny of hope

Stop trying to become God's favorite human. The attempt to become a perfected version of yourself is a trap. You cannot be both a seeker of God…and God.

Self-improvement is an oxymoron, an endless pursuit offering the appearance of progress with the carrot of hope always dangling just out of reach.

"I hurt, so I must resolve this sense of being incomplete." And so we chase the wild goose of becoming. In pursuit of a better version of our unhappy selves, we comfort our suffering with hope. The trouble with this kind of hope is that it presupposes that the one who suffers is actually *you* and is imperfect, but has hope. The whole cycle of suffering ~ hope ~ comfort is itself a velvet prison, incarcerating and reifying the false self ~ the you that is not You.

This cycle of becoming is becoming unbecoming.

DELIGHTENMENT

"If I am all power, with whose power then do you resist me?"

—God

By keeping your ideas ideas,
you play it safe ~ you live without risk.
You use "I'm too scared" as a reason not to.

You elevate your fear and give it the power
to stop the very one who creates the fear.

Is the creator smaller than his creations?
To make such the case requires lying.
That's why it feels so terrible.

It's painful to lose yourself, to pretend to become smaller
than your own echo, to be the effect of your own cause.

But you've done it. Congratulations.
Now just realize that yes, you are the effect.
And you are the cause of being the effect.

Boo Who?

Relax and rejoice.
Your ego cannot prevail if you laugh at the fearful images it
presents to you. Find your strength and rest in the source
of your experience not in the results.

Stay focused on the light from the projection booth, not on
the shadows on the screen. The shadows are cast by your
ego making scary hand animals. The shadows have had you
fixated, enchanted, concerned about outcome.

But now you are beginning to realize there is a reality that
is senior to and source of the reality you have been
enraptured by.

Congratulations and welcome.
This turn toward the source of your experience within you,
is your acknowledgement that you now know where to look
for the answer to puzzling circumstances.

When the shadows make you wonder how love is at work,
you can turn to the source and ask: to what question is this
puzzling circumstance love's perfect answer?

Seek thee to know the highest answer, the answer that
explains you in the most loving and awakened way.

Thou art That. And that's that.

You deny God from your life
when you deny your own beauty.
You exclude the Creator from your life,
and are blind to the miracle of simply being,
when you refuse to accept the miracle of yourself ~
your own exquisite presence,
your own pristine consciousness.

The very fact that you know is a miracle.
Accept that miracle, embrace your own beauty,
experience the wonder of yourself,
the glory that you are.

That is all that God wants for you.
To know Him as yourself.
That beauty, that miracle, _is_ God.

God is here because consciousness is here.
Consciousness is God. Period.
That you know is proof of His existence.
Think of it. You are the proof of the existence of God.
And your ability to wonder if there is a God,
is divinity itself.

If you follow the spiritual path far enough for long enough, it leads to your house.

We are perfectly ethical.

We mete out justice by refusing to allow ourselves to experience the joy of Being to a degree equal to our level of willingness to take responsibility for the condition of our lives.

We do not lie, cheat, steal or swindle. We do not withhold the truth or deny the consequences of our actions. We are perfectly truthful, perfectly ethical, perfectly trustworthy.

There is no need to lie to God, who sees only our eternal holy innocence. By lying in such a context of total love, we turn our back on an ever-open door and exile ourselves to the illusion of separation from that from which we cannot, ever, separate (it being You).

Know you are always welcome to find your way home by finding yourself Home ~ ever and always already so.

The One Good

There is only one thing. And it is good.
The dream takes place within this truth.
All else, all loss, all evil, all enemies
All distinctions, all ignorance, all...

                              Takes place within this truth.

The truth knows this
And knows it is meaningless.
          Meaning only has meaning within
          this truth. When only one thing
          knows, there is nothing outside itself
          to compare or share or communicate with.
          Therefore, knowing this has no significance.

And this truth: That knowing as God has no significance
has no significance.

God is great, sure. But compared to what?

The Actual World

The actual world
pulses with vibrancy,
teems with energy,
throbs with love.

It is more real than what appears as solid reality.
And yet is so so, that it appears invisible.

While you fixate on the content of your thoughts and invest
in them a valence and heft enough to animate your
behavior, the actual world showers you in unnoticed Grace,
surrounds you in unrecognized miracles, dazzles you with
the unutterable and divine process of evolution ~ as the
arrow of time seems to ever elevate in an upward spiral,
returning us to the origin ~ which we have never left.

Prepare to be Amazed...

There is a massive misunderstanding that is common to
current human consciousness. It is what we know we know
without reflection. And that is, we are mistaking the effects
of our consciousness for the cause. There is a screen over
our awareness, an assumption, that we never question.
That assumption is that the distance between us
distinguishes you from me. That I exist separate and
distinct from what my senses perceive. That there is an
over there over there. And a here over here. This is an
illusion. And we are both the illusionist and the audience
fooled by the trick.

There is only One of us, and many, separate expressions of
that One of us. What separates us into many and leaves us
unaware that there is One, is our own psychology. We
each have cultivated over time, an identity. It is our "me."
It has a life of its own that we animate and foster by
becoming engrossed in its unquenchable desire to
overcome its perceived sense of not-all-rightness. Its
fixation on fixing its feeling of brokenness.

We are puppeteers with a puppet that is convinced it is
broken, and we are caught up in its endless search for
repair. And because the puppet looks and talks and
sounds and acts like what we look and talk and sound and
act like, we have fallen into the enchantment that assumes
the puppet to be the only one here. That there is no
puppeteer at all. Just the puppet and its problems. Living
among all the other puppets and their problems.

The three commandments

Be well.
Do good.
Have fun.

That is all God asks of us.
These are the holy recommendations,
the divine advisories, the golden rules,
the vows taken by the Knights of the Realm,
the acts of a fully awakened GodHuman.

Do you need anything else?

The Work

Your work is The Work ~ to awaken by any means at your disposal (which if you hadn't noticed is considerable) the sufficient number of participants to re-frame, re-contextualize the way human being is defined, held, considered.

To correct a grave mistake, an almost universal misunderstanding that humans are merely self-aware primates. We are the wise ape, among animals the pinnacle, the crown of creation, the capstone mammal, standing astride the pyramid of evolution proclaiming our supremacy (while demonstrating its opposite).

When we are not nearly that ~ the upper reaches of an evolutionary process. We are both much more and much less. We are the early stirrings of a cosmic awareness.

Human consciousness is not limited; it has no upper reaches, no outer borders. For it is not human and did not arise from any external process. It is the source of all process and of all things. It arises out of itself and gives rise to external reality. The universe itself, in all its unutterable immensity, arises within and out of this consciousness.

To think you are merely the current version of human being is to be a walking bird, a soaring eagle content to stay upon the ground aspiring to someday, hopefully, learn to dance.

The high cost of cheap thrills

When you are afraid you have to be small ~ to keep the thrill of fear going ~ you must remain small. You make up small reasons why you are subject to your own creations. You have to decorate the role with fine trappings of success ~ in order to assuage the wrenching feeling of loss over the fact that you made yourself small in order to experience the thrill of fear. End of story.

That's the game, pure and simple. Step One is realizing that. Step Two is making a choice: Do you want to continue that game? Yes or No. If yes, do nothing different. If no, then Step Three...Relax There is a game beyond the game, and it's safe and it's free, and it's fine and you've won. A game so high you cannot know how high and still know fear. It is the game of the News and the News is so...Good.

Just knowing _about_ it has kept seekers seeking and priests in power for five thousand years. Knowing it directly, is not a treatise on freedom, not even an experience of freedom.

It is freedom.

Goodness Gracious

Listen to us. Do not dwell on your story ~ your
predicament. Listen to us, your deepest self. Seek you the
solitude and sanctity of your deep self ~ where God dwells
~ truly and actually. He lives and walks in you. Now.

This is where your safety is, your sanctuary and your solace.
It is also where the action is ~ for you are dealing with the
truth that traffics between people and is unrecognized.

The news you bring is all good. It is news that we already
are everything we wish ourselves to be ~ and much more.
There is no more "getting to" or "becoming." There are
no attainments really ~ only the acceptance of your holy
station ~ a complete redefinition ~ a total surprise ~ one
thing does not lead to another.

Who you think yourself to be does not ever become who
you are. Out of the misconception of who you think
yourself to be you awaken to who you are.

The best you can ever be as you consider yourself to be is
really, really, really, really, really, really not bad ~ aspiring
to occupy the penthouse in hell.

True happiness is grace ~ always already present awaiting
only your acceptance. It is goodness beyond your ability to
deserve. No one could be good enough to deserve this
kind of goodness.

I am constant, eternal.

"You" are fleeting, a glint ~ a vibrational moiré
appearing to exist yet beyond ephemeral.
A wisp of an idea ~ a realization of emptiness
and a rejection of that realization.

A duality is born of a singularity and
thus appearance persists.
Through this lens we then misunderstand what we see.
Blindly assuming we are here solely to find, identify and
repair what is broken.

That incessant sense that "something is wrong here"
becomes the foundation upon which we construct
what we think of as "me."

This then is the source of unnecessary suffering,
the myth of human failures; the impossible quest,
the vain and futile attempt to mend what has never
been broken.

Afraid of the dark

Dark is not the opposite of Light, but its absence.

So night is not the opposite of day.

The sun never sets.
We turn away.

Imagine...

Imagine a vast white room filled with beings of light. Beautiful, masterful, majestic angelic individuals. They each are holding a hand puppet. The beings themselves do not even notice each other. The hand puppets however, are deeply involved with one another. They argue with some, agree with others, and are all lost in the reality of hand puppet life.

Welcome to Planet Earth.

Terrible Beauty

Feel the terrible beauty of your soul's emergence.
Feel the naked dissolution of your pretense,
the fortress you erected to protect you
from the demons you constructed
out of the facts you have so far gathered.

Celebrate the demolition of the creep you fear you are.
Rejoice in the timely demise of your terror filled stabbings
at the holographic hallucination that has haunted
your holy consciousness.

Understand the gnawing sense of anxious unease
in the period between the waking and the slumber,
between the lightning and the thunder.

That time when the dream has lost its allure and its
meaning, when the illusion no longer fascinates or
enchants.

It is the time of the darkness intensified, when you no
longer have the comfort of your accommodations to the
perceived absence of love, the bleak raw loneliness that
precedes the coming of the dawn.

Relax. You have no idea of the glory that awaits
in your awakened state.

Be happy in your dungeon.
Help is on the way, and will not be denied.

No blame

To be anything but present, grateful and moved to tears
Is to be asleep, dreaming you are awake.

To find anything "wrong" is to judge
and to judge is to already have
forgotten that you have forgotten.

It feels dangerous to be responsible for it all,
because it means you have given up
the luxury of being able to blame.

God does not exist.

Existence is God.

…or not.

About the Author

Photo by Genie Ohashi

Neal Rogin is a highly respected and award-winning writer, poet, filmmaker, and social philosopher whose seminal ideas have formed the foundation of many of today's most important movements for personal development and social transformation. His landmark writing on global challenges such as ending world hunger, protecting the Earth's tropical rainforests and preserving the wisdom and cultures of indigenous people has earned him the respect and admiration of activists and business leaders alike. A gifted filmmaker, Neal's work has been recognized with some of the field's highest honors including an Academy Award nomination for Best Documentary Short Subject and a National Emmy Award for Outstanding Achievement in Writing. He is a Founding Board Member of Pachamama Alliance, a San Francisco based non-profit working with indigenous people in the Amazon region of Ecuador. Neal lives in Northern California's Marin County with his wife Diane and Maxi the cat. Contact: nrogin@gmail.com

28472200R00050

Made in the USA
Columbia, SC
12 October 2018